THE WAR OF THE WENUSES

Translated from the Artesian of

H. G. POZZUOLI

AUTHOR OF "THE TREADMILL," "THE ISTHMUS OF DR. DAY"
"THE VANISHING LADY," ETC., ETC.

BY

C. L. GRAVES AND E. V. LUCAS

"Not novels and poetry swipes, but ideas, science, books"
The Artilleryman

Arrowsmith's Bristol Library
Vol. LXXVIII.

All rights reversed

TO
H. G. WELLS
THIS OUTRAGE
ON A FASCINATING AND CONVINCING
ROMANCE

CONTENTS.

Book I.—The Coming of the Wenuses.

Chap.		Page
I.	"JUST BEFORE THE BATTLE, MOTHER"	11
II.	THE FALLING STAR	22
III.	THE CRINOLINE EXPANDS	34
IV.	HOW I REACHED HOME	46

Book II.—London Under the Wenuses.

I.	THE DEATH OF THE EXAMINER	63
II.	THE MAN AT UXBRIDGE ROAD	81
III.	THE TEA-TRAY IN WESTBOURNE GROVE	95
IV.	WRECKAGE	109
V.	BUBBLES	117

Appendix A 127

Appendix B 137

Book I.

The Coming of the Wenuses.

The Coming of the Wemuses.

I.

"JUST BEFORE THE BATTLE, MOTHER."

NO one would have believed in the first years of the twentieth century that men and modistes on this planet were being watched by intelligences greater than woman's and yet as ambitious as her own. With infinite complacency maids and matrons went to and fro over London, serene in the assurance of their empire over man. It is possible that the mysticetus does the same. Not one of them gave a thought to Wenus as a source of danger, or thought of it only to dismiss the idea of active rivalry upon it as impossible or improbable. Yet across the gulf of space astral women, with eyes that are to the eyes of English women as diamonds are to boot-buttons, astral women, with hearts vast and warm and sympathetic, were regarding Butterick's with envy, Peter Robinson's with jealousy, and Whiteley's with insatiable yearning, and

"Just before the battle, Mother." 13

slowly and surely maturing their plans for a grand inter-stellar campaign.

The pale pink planet Wenus, as I need hardly inform the sober reader, revolves round the sun at a mean distance of ♀ vermillion miles. More than that, as has been proved by the recent observations of Puits of Paris, its orbit is steadily but surely advancing sunward. That is to say, it is rapidly becoming too hot for clothes to be worn at all; and this, to the Wenuses, was so alarming a prospect that the immediate problem of life became the discovery of new quarters notable for a gentler climate and more copious fashions. The last stage of struggle-for-dress, which is to us still remote, had embellished their charms, heightened their heels and enlarged their hearts. Moreover, the population of Wenus consisted exclusively of Invisible Men—and the Wenuses were about tired of it. Let us, however, not judge them too harshly. Remember what ruthless havoc our own species has wrought, not only on animals such as the Moa and the Maori, but upon its own inferior races such as the Wanishing Lady and the Dodo Bensonii.

The Wenuses seem to have calculated

their descent with quite un-feminine accuracy. Had our instruments permitted it, we might have witnessed their preparations. Similarly pigs, had they wings, might fly. Men like Quellen of Dresden watched the pale pink planet —it is odd, by the way, that for countless centuries Wenus has been the star of Eve—evening by evening growing alternately paler and pinker than a literary agent, but failed to interpret the extraordinary phenomena, resembling a series of powder puffs, which he observed issuing from the cardiac penumbra on the night of April 1st, 1902. At the same time a great light was remarked by Idos of Yokohama and Pegadiadis of Athens.

The storm burst upon us six weeks later, about the time of the summer sales. As Wenus approached opposition, Dr. Jelli of Guava set the wires of the astronomical exchange palpitating with the intelligence of a huge explosion of laughing gas moving risibly towards the earth. He compared it to a colossal cosmic cachinnation. And, in the light of subsequent events, the justice of the comparison will commend itself to all but the most sober readers.

Had it not been for my chance meeting with Swears, the eminent

"*Just before the battle, Mother.*" 17

astronomer and objurgationist, this book would never have been written. He asked me down to our basement, which he rents from me as an observatory, and in spite of all that has happened since I still remember our wigil very distinctly. (I spell it with a "w" from an inordinate affection for that letter.) Swears moved about, invisible but painfully audible to my naked ear. The night was very warm, and I was very thirsty. As I gazed through the syphon, the little star seemed alternately to expand and contract, and finally to assume a sort of dual skirt, but that was simply because my eye was tired. I remember how I sat under the table with patches of green and crimson swimming before my eyes. Grotesque and foolish as this may seem to the sober reader, it is absolutely true.

Swears watched till one, and then he gave it up. He was full of speculations about the condition of Wenus. Swears' language was extremely sultry.

"The chances against anything ladylike on Wenus," he said, "are a million to one."

Even *Pearson's Weekly* woke up to the disturbance at last, and Mrs. Lynn

Linton contributed an article entitled "What Women Might Do" to the *Queen*. A paper called *Punch*, if I remember the name aright, made a pun on the subject, which was partially intelligible with the aid of italics and the laryngoscope. For my own part, I was too much occupied in teaching my wife to ride a Bantam, and too busy upon a series of papers in *Nature* on the turpitude of the classical professoriate of the University of London, to give my undivided attention to the impending disaster. I cannot divide things easily; I am an indivisible man. But one night I went for a bicycle ride with my wife. She *was* a Bantam of delight, I can tell you, but she rode very badly. It was starlight, and I was attempting to explain the joke in the paper called, if I recollect aright, *Punch*. It was an extraordinarily sultry night, and I told her the names of all the stars she saw as she fell off her machine. She had a good bulk of falls. There were lights in the upper windows of the houses as the people went to bed. Grotesque and foolish as this will seem to the sober reader, it is absolutely true. Coming home, a party of bean-feasters from Wimbledon, Wormwood Scrubs, or Woking passed us, singing and playing concertinas. It all seemed so safe and tranquil. But the Wenuses were even then on their milky way.

II.

THE FALLING STAR.

THEN came the night of the first star. It was seen early in the morning rushing over Winchester; leaving a gentle frou-frou behind it. Trelawny, of the Wells' Observatory, the greatest authority on Meteoric Crinolines, watched it anxiously. Winymann, the publisher, who sprang to fame by the publication of *The War of the Worlds*, saw it from his office window, and at once telegraphed to me: " Materials for new

The Falling Star. 23

book in the air." That was the first hint I received of the wonderful wisit. I lived in those days at 181a Campden Hill Gardens. It is the house opposite the third lamp-post on the right as you walk east. It was of brick and slate, with a party-wall, and two spikes were wanting to the iron railings. When the telegram came I was sitting in my study writing a discussion on the atomic theory of Krelli of Balmoral. I at once changed the Woking jacket in which I was writing for evening dress—which wanted, I remember, a button—and hastened to the Park. I did not tell my wife anything about it. I did not care to have her with me. In all such adventures I find her more useful as a sentimental figure in the background—I, of course, allow no sentiment in the foreground—than an active participant.

On the way I met Swears, returning from breakfast with our mutual friend, Professor Heat Ray Lankester—they had had Lee-Metford sardines and Cairns marmalade, he told me,—and we sought the meteor together.

Find it we did in Kensington Gardens. An enormous dimple had been made by the impact of the projectile, which lay almost buried in the earth. Two or three trees, broken by its fall, sprawled on the turf. Among this *débris* was the missile; resembling nothing so much as a huge crinoline. At the moment we reached the spot P.C. A 581 was ordering it off; and Henry Pearson, aged 28 (no fixed abode), and Martha Griffin, aged 54, of Maybury Tenements, were circulating among the crowd offering matches for sale. They have nothing to do with this story, but their names and addresses make for verisimilitude; or at least, I hope so. In case they do not, let me add that Mary Griffin wore a blue peignoir which had seen better days, and Herbert Pearson's matches struck everywhere except on the box.

With a mental flash we linked the Crinoline with the powder puffs on Wenus. Approaching it more nearly, we heard a hissing noise within, such as is made by an ostler, or Mr. Daimler grooming his motor car.

"Good heavens!" said Swears, "there's a horse in it. Can't you hear? He must be half-roasted."

So saying he rushed off, fraught with pity, to inform the Secretary of the Society for the Prevention of Cruelty to Animals; while I hurried away to tell Pendriver the journalist, proposing in my own mind, I recollect, that he should give me half the profits on the article.

Pendriver the journalist, so called to distinguish him from Hoopdriver the cyclist, was working in his garden. He does the horticultural column for one of the large dailies.

"You've read about the disturbances in Venus?" I cried.

"What!" said Pendriver. He is as deaf as the *Post*, the paper he writes for.

"You've read about Venus?" I asked again.

"No," he said, "I've never been to Venice."

"Venus!" I bawled, "Venus!"

"Yes," said Pendriver, "Venus. What about it?"

"Why," I said, "there are people from Venus in Kensington Gardens."

"Venus in Kensington Gardens!" he replied. "No, it's not Venus; it's the Queen."

I began to get angry.

"Not the statue," I shouted. "Wisitors from Wenus. Make copy. Come and see! Copy! Copy!"

The word "copy" galvanised him, and he came, spade and all. We quickly crossed the Park once more. Pendriver lives to the west of it, in Strathmore Gardens, and has a special permit from his landlord to dig. We did not, for sufficient reasons, converse much. Many persons were now hastening towards the strange object. Among them I noticed Jubal Gregg the butcher (who fortunately did not observe me—we owed him a trifle of eighteen shillings, and had since taken to Canterbury lamb from the Colonial Meat Stores), and a jobbing gardener, whom I had not recently paid. I forget his name, but he was lame in the left leg: a ruddy man.

Quite a crowd surrounded the Crinoline when we arrived, and in addition to the match-vendors already mentioned, there was now Giuseppe Mandolini, from Leather Lane, with an accordion and a monkey. Monkeys are of course forbidden in Kensington Gardens, and how he eluded the police I cannot imagine. Most of the people were staring quietly at the Crinoline, totally unaware of its significance. Scientific knowledge has not progressed at Kensington by the same leaps and bounds as at Woking. Extra-terrestrial had less meaning for them than extra-special.

We found Swears hard at work keeping the crowd from touching the Crinoline. With him was a tall, red-haired man, who I afterwards learnt was Lee-Bigge, the Secretary of the Society for the Prevention of Cruelty to Animals. He had a summons and several officials with him, and was standing on the Crinoline, bellowing directions in a clear, rich voice, occasionally impeded by emotion, like an ox with a hiccough.

As soon as Swears saw me, he asked me to bring a policeman to assist him to keep back the crowd; and I went away, proud to be so honoured, to find one. I was unsuccessful. P.C. A581 had gone off duty; but another constable, I was told, had been seen, an hour or so earlier, asleep against the railings,—it was a baker's boy who told me, just back from delivering muffins in St. Mary Abbot's Terrace,— and had since wandered in the direction of the Albert Hall. I followed, but could not see him in any of the areas, and therefore returned slowly by way of Queen's Gate, Cromwell Road, Earl's Court Road, and Kensington High Street, hoping to meet another; and as it was then about noon, I entered an A.B.C. and had half a pork-pie and a bucket of Dr. Jaeger's Vi-cocolate. I remember the circumstance distinctly, because feeling rather hungry and wishing to vary the *menu*, I asked the girl for half a veal-and-ham pie and she brought me the balance of the original pasty; and when I remonstrated, she said that her directors recognised no essential difference between veal-and-ham and pork.

III.

THE CRINOLINE EXPANDS.

WHEN I returned to the Gardens the sun was at his zenith. The crowd around the Crinoline had increased and some sort of a struggle seemed to be going on. As I drew near I heard Lee-Bigge's voice:

"Keep back! keep back!"

A boy came running towards me.

"It's a-movin'," he said to me as he passed; "a-blowin' and a-blowin' out. Now we shan't be long!"

The Crinoline Expands.

Passing on, I saw that it was indeed expanding. The ribs were more distended and the covering more tightly stretched. The hissing had ceased and a creaking noise had taken its place. There was evidently great pressure within. Once something resembling an *en tout cas* was thrust through the top, making what was presumably an attempt to dislodge Lee-Bigge, and then suddenly the Crinoline burst, revealing a wision of ultra-mundane loveliness.

I shall not attempt exhaustively to describe the indescribable. It is enough to assure the sober reader that, grotesque and foolish as it may seem, this is absolutely true, and to record that after the glimpse I had of the Wenuses emerging from the Crinoline in which they had come to the earth from their planet, a kind of fascination paralysed my actions. All other men in the crowd seemed to be similarly affected. We were battle-grounds of love and curiosity. For the Wenuses were gorgeous : that is the sum of the matter.

Those who have never seen a living Wenus (there is a specimen in fairly good spirits in the Natural History Museum) can scarcely imagine the strange beauty of their appearance. The peculiar W-shaped mouth, the incessant nictitation of the sinister eyelid, the naughty little twinkle in the eye itself, the glistening glory of the arms, each terminating in a fleshy digitated Handling Machine resembling more than anything else a Number 6 glove inflated with air (these members, by the way, have since been named rather aptly by that distinguished anatomist and original dog, Professor Howes, the *hands*)—all combined to produce an effect akin to stupefaction. I stood there ecstatic, unprogressive, immoderate; while swiftly and surely ungovernable affection for all Wenuses gripped me.

Meanwhile I heard inarticulate exclamations on all sides.

"Shameless hussies!" cried a woman near me.

"By Jove, that's something like!" said a young man who had been reading Captain Coe's finals, swinging round towards the Crinoline, with one foot arrested in mid-air.

My inclination when I recovered partial self-possession was to make instantly for the Crinoline and avow my devotion and allegiance, but at that moment I caught the eye of my wife, who had followed me to the Park, and I hastily turned my back on the centre of attraction. I saw, however, that Pendriver was using his spade to cleave his way to the Wenuses; and Swears was standing on the brink of the pit transfixed with adoration; while a young shopman from Woking, in town for the day, completely lost his head. It came bobbing over the grass to my very feet; but I remembered the experiences of Pollock and the Porroh man and let it go.

The news of our visitors seemed to have spread by some subtle magic, for in every direction I could see nothing but running men, some with women pulling at their sleeves and coat-tails to detain them, advancing by great strides towards us. Even a policeman was among them, rubbing his eyes. My wife broke through the crowd and grasped me firmly by the arm.

"Pozzy," she said, "this is my opportunity and I mean to use it. I was kept doing nothing between pages 68 and 296 of the other book, and this time I mean to work. Look at these fools rushing to their doom. In another moment they will be mashed, mashed to jelly; and you too, unless I prevent it. I know what these Wenuses are.

Haven't I had a scientific training? You will be mashed, I tell you—mashed!"

So saying she banged on the ground with her umbrella, which, I remember now with sorrow, we had bought the week before at Derry and Toms' for five-and-eleven-three.

Meanwhile a few of the men had to some extent recovered, and headed by the R.S.P.C.A. Secretary had formed a deputation, and were busy talking on their fingers to the Wenuses. But the Wenuses were too much occupied in dropping into each other's eyes something from a bright flask, which I took to be Beggarstaffs' Elect Belladonna, to heed them.

I turned in response to a tug at my swallow-tails from my wife, and when I looked again a row of Wenuses with closed lids stood before the Crinoline. Suddenly they opened their eyes and flashed them on the men before them. The effect was instantaneous. The deputation, as the glance touched them, fell like skittles—viscous, protoplasmic masses, victims of the terrible Mash-Glance of the Wenuses.

I attributed my own escape to the prompt action of my wife, who stood before and shielded me, for upon women the Mash-Glance had no effect. The ray must have missed me only by a second, for my elbow which was not wholly covered by my wife's bulk was scorched, and my hat has never since recovered its pristine gloss. Turning, I saw a bus-driver in Knightsbridge leap up and explode, while his conductor clutched at the rail, missed it and fell overboard; farther still, on the distant horizon, the bricklayers on a gigantic scaffolding went off bang against the lemon-yellow of the sky as the glance reached them, and the Bachelors' Club at Albert Gate fell with a crash. All this had happened with such swiftness that I was dumbfounded. Then, after a few moments, my wife slowly and reluctantly stepped aside and allowed me to survey the scene. The Wenuses, having scored their first victory, once more had retired into the recesses of the Crinoline. The ground for some distance was littered with the bodies of the mashed; I alone among men stood erect, my conscious companions being a sprinkling of women, pictures of ungovernable fury.

Yet my feeling was not one of joy at my escape. Strange mind of man!—instead, even with the Wenuses' victims lying all around me, my heart went out to the Crinoline and its astral occupants. I, too, wished to be mashed. And suddenly I was aware that my wife knew that I was thinking thus. With an effort I turned and began a stumbling run through the Park.

IV.

HOW I REACHED HOME.

I REMEMBER nothing of my flight, except the stress of blundering against trees and stumbling over the railings. To blunder against some trees is very stressful. At last I could go no further: I had run full tilt into a gasworks. I fell and lay still.

I must have remained there some time.

Suddenly, like a thing falling upon

me from without, came—Beer. It was being poured down my throat by my cousin's man, and I recollect thinking that he must have used the same can with which he filled the lamps. How he got there I cannot pretend to tell.

"What news from the park?" said I.

"Eh!" said my cousin's man.

"What news from the Park?" I said.

"Garn! 'oo yer getting at?" said my cousin's man. "Aint yer just *been* there?" (The italics are his own.) "People seem fair silly abart the Pawk. Wot's it all abart?"

"Haven't you heard of the Wenuses?" said I. "The women from Wenus?"

"Quite enough," said my cousin's man, and laughed.

I felt foolish and angry.

"You'll hear more yet," I said, and went on my way.

Judging by the names of the streets, I seemed to be at Kennington, and it was an hour after dawn, and my collar had burst away from its stud. But I had ceased to feel fear. My terror had fallen from me like a bath towel. Three things struggled for the possession of my mind: the beauty of Kennington, the whereabouts of the Wenuses, and the wengeance of my wife. In spite of my cousin's man's beer, which I could still taste, I was ravenously hungry; so, seeing no one about, I broke into a chemist's shop and stayed the pangs on a cake of petroleum soap, some Parrish's food, and a box of menthol pastilles, which I washed down with a split ammoniated quinine and Condy. I then stole across the road, and dragging the cushions from a deserted cab (No. 8648) into the cab shelter, I snatched a few more hours of restless sleep.

When I woke I found myself thinking consecutively, a thing I do not remember to have done since I killed the curate in the other book. In the interim my mental condition had been chaotic, asymptotic. But during slumber my brain, incredible as it may seem, stimulated and clarified by the condiments of which I had partaken, had resumed its normal activity. I determined to go home.

Resolving at any cost to reach Campden Hill Gardens by a sufficiently circuitous route, I traversed Kennington Park Road, Newington Butts, Newington Causeway, Blackman Street, and the Borough High Street, to London Bridge. Crossing the bridge, I met a newspaper boy with a bundle of papers, still wet from the press. They were halfpenny copies of the *Star*, but he charged me a penny for mine. The imposition still rankles.

From it I learned that a huge cordon of police, which had been drawn round the Crinoline, had been mashed beyond recognition, and two regiments of Life Guards razed to the ground, by the devastating Glance of the Wenuses. I passed along King William Street and Prince's Street to Moorgate Street. Here I met another newspaper boy, carrying the *Pall Mall Gazette*. I handed him a threepenny bit; but though I waited for twenty minutes, he offered me no change. This will give some idea of the excitement then beginning to prevail. The *Pall Mall* had an article on the situation, which I read as I climbed the City Road' to Islington. It stated that Mrs. Pozzuoli, my wife, had constituted herself Commander-in-Chief, and was busy marshalling her forces. I was relieved by the news, for it suggested that my wife was fully occupied. Already a good bulk of nursemaids and cooks, enraged at the destruction of the Scotland Yard and Knightsbridge heroes by the Wenuses' Mash-Glance, had joined her flag. It was, said the *Pall Mall*, high time that such an attack was undertaken, and since women had been proved to be immune to the Mash-

Glance, it was clearly their business to undertake it.

Meanwhile, said the *Pall Mall*, nothing could check the folly of the men. Like moths to a candle, so were they hastening to Kensington Gardens, only to be added to the heap of mashed that already had accumulated there.

So far, the *P. M. G.* But my mother, who was in the thick of events at the time, has since given me fuller particulars. Notwithstanding, my mother tells me, the fate of their companions, the remainder of the constabulary and military forces stationed in London hastened to the Park, impelled by the fearful fascination, and were added to the piles of mashed.

Afterwards came the Volunteers, to a man, and then the Cloth. The haste of most of the curates, and a few bishops whose names have escaped me, was, said my mother, cataclysmic. Old dandies with creaking joints tottered along Piccadilly to their certain doom; young clerks in the city, explaining that they wished to attend their aunt's funeral, crowded the omnibuses for Kensington and were seen no more; while my mother tells me that excursion trains from the country were arriving at the principal stations throughout the day, bearing huge loads of provincial inamorati.

A constant stream of infatuated men, flowing from east to west, set in, and though bands of devoted women formed barriers across the principal thoroughfares for the purpose of barring their progress, no perceptible check was effected. Once, a Judge of notable austerity was observed to take to a lamp-post to avoid detention by his wife: once, a well-known tenor turned down by a by-street, says my mother, pursued by no fewer than fifty-seven admirers burning to avert his elimination. Members of Parliament surged across St. James' Park and up Constitution Hill.

Yet in every walk of life, says my mother, there were a few survivors in the shape of stolid, adamantine misogynists.

Continuing my journey homewards, I traversed Upper Street, Islington, and the Holloway Road to Highgate Hill, which I ascended at a sharp run. At the summit I met another newspaper boy carrying a bundle of *Globes*, one of which I purchased, after a hard-driven bargain, for two shillings and a stud from the shirt-front of my evening dress, which was beginning to show signs of ennui. I leaned against the wall of the Highgate Literary and Scientific Institute, to read it. The news was catastrophic. Commander Wells of the Fire Brigade had, it stated, visited Kensington Gardens with two manuals, one steam engine, and a mile of hose, in order to play upon the Crinoline and its occupants. Presuming on the immunity of persons bearing his name during the Martian invasion, the gallant Commander had approached too near and was in a moment reduced to salvage.

Pondering on this news, I made for Parliament Hill, by way of West Hill and Milfield Lane. On the top I paused to survey London at my feet, and, to get the fullest benefit of the invigorating breeze, removed my hat. But the instant I did so, I was aware of a sharp pain on my scalp and the aroma of singed hair. Lifting my hand to the wounded place, I discovered that I had been shaved perfectly clean, as with a Heat Razor. The truth rushed upon me: I had come within the range of the Mash-Glance, and had been saved from total dissolution only by intervening masonry protecting my face and body.

To leave the Hill was the work of an

instant. I passed through John Street to Hampstead Road, along Belsize Avenue and Buckland Crescent to Belsize Road, and so to Canterbury Road and Kilburn Lane. Here I met a fourth newspaper boy loaded with copies of the *St. James' Gazette.* He offered me one for seven-and-sixpence, or two for half a sovereign, but it seemed to me I had read enough.

Turning into Ladbroke Grove Road I quickly reached Notting Hill, and stealthily entered my house in Campden Hill Gardens ten minutes later.

Book II.

London under the Wenuses.

London under the Wenuses.

I.

THE DEATH OF THE EXAMINER.

MY first act on entering my house, in order to guard against any sudden irruption on the part of my wife, was to bolt the door and put on the chain. My next was to visit the pantry, the cellar, and the larder, but they were all void of food and drink. My wife must have been there first. As I had drunk nothing since I burgled the Kennington chemist's, I was very thirsty, though my mind was still hydrostatic. I cannot account for it on scientific principles, but I felt very angry with my wife. Suddenly I was struck by a happy thought, and hurrying upstairs I found a bottle of methylated spirits on my wife's toilet-table. Strange as it may seem to the sober reader, I drank greedily of the unfamiliar beverage, and feeling refreshed and thoroughly kinetic, settled down once more to an exhaustive exposure of the dishonest off-handedness of the external Examiners at University College. I

The Death of the Examiner.

may add that I had taken the bread-knife (by Mappin) from the pantry, as it promised to be useful in the case of unforeseen Clerical emergencies. I should have preferred the meat-chopper with which the curate had been despatched in *The War of the Worlds*, but it was deposited in the South Kensington Museum along with other mementoes of the Martian invasion. Besides, my wife and I had both become Wegetarians.

The evening was still, and though distracted at times by recollections of the Wenuses, I made good progress with my indictment. Suddenly I was conscious of a pale pink glow which suffused my writing-pad, and I heard a soft but unmistakable thud as of a pinguid body falling in the immediate vicinity.

Taking off my boots, I stole gently down to the scullery and applied the spectroscope to the keyhole. To my mingled amazement and ecstasy, I perceived a large dome-shaped fabric blocking up the entire back garden. Roughly speaking, it seemed to be about the size of a full-grown sperm whale. A faint heaving was perceptible in the mass, and further evidences of vitality were forthcoming in a gentle but pathetic crooning, as of an immature chimæra booming in the void. The truth flashed upon me in a moment. The Second Crinoline had fallen in my back garden.

My mind was instantly made up. To expose myself unarmed to the fascination of the Wonderful Wisitors would have irreparably prejudiced the best interests of scientific research. My only hope lay in a complete disguise which should enable me to pursue my investigations of the Wenuses with the minimum amount of risk. A student of the humanities would have adopted a different method, but my standpoint has always been dispassionate, anti-sentimental. My feelings towards the Wenuses were, incredible as it may seem, purely Platonic. I recognised their transcendental attractions, but had no desire to succumb to them. Strange as it may seem, the man who succumbs rarely if ever is victorious in the long run. To disguise my sex and identity—for it was *a priori* almost impossible that the inhabitants of Wenus had never heard of Pozzuoli —would guard me from the jellifying Mash-Glance of the Wenuses. Arrayed in feminine garb I could remain immune to their malignant influences.

With me, to think is to act; so I hastily ran upstairs, shaved off my moustache, donned my wife's bicycle-skirt, threw her *sortie de bal* round my shoulders, borrowed the cook's Sunday bonnet from the servants' bedroom, and hastened back to my post of observation at the scullery door. Inserting a pipette through the keyhole and cautiously applying my eye, I saw to my delight that the Crinoline had been elevated on a series of steel rods about six feet high, and that the five Wenuses who had descended in it were partaking of a light but sumptuous repast beneath its iridescent canopy.

They were seated round a tripod imbibing a brown beverage from small vessels resembling the half of a hollow sphere, and eating with incredible velocity a quantity of tiny round coloured objects—closely related, as I subsequently had occasion to ascertain, to the *Bellaria angelica*—which they raised to their mouths with astonishing and unerring aim in the complex Handling-Machines, or Tenticklers, which form part of their wonderful organism.

Belonging as they undoubtedly do to the order of the Tunicates, their exquisitely appropriate and elegant

The Death of the Examiner. 71

costume may be safely allowed to speak for itself. It is enough, however, to note the curious fact that there are no buttons in Wenus, and that their mechanical system is remarkable, incredible as it may seem, for having developed the eye to the rarest point of perfection while dispensing entirely with the hook. The bare idea of this is no doubt terribly repulsive to us, but at the same time I think we should remember how indescribably repulsive our sartorial habits must seem to an intelligent armadillo.

Of the peculiar coralline tint of the Wenuses' complexion, I think I have already spoken. That it was developed by their indulgence in the Red Weed has been, I think, satisfactorily proved by the researches of Dr. Moreau, who also shows that the visual range of their eyes was much the same as ours, except that blue and yellow were alike to them. Moreau established this by a very pretty experiment with a Yellow Book and a Blue Book, each of which elicited exactly the same remark, a curious hooting sound, strangely resembling the *ut de poitrine* of one of Professor Garner's gorillas.

After concluding their repast, the Wenuses, still unaware of my patient scrutiny, extracted, with the aid of their glittering tintackles, a large packet of Red Weed from a quasi-marsupial pouch in the roof of the Crinoline, and in an incredibly short space of time had rolled its carmine tendrils into slim cylinders, and inserted them within their lips. The external ends suddenly ignited as though by spontaneous combustion; but in reality that result was effected by the simple process of deflecting the optic ray. Clouds of roseate vapour, ascending to the dome of the canopy, partially obscured the sumptuous contours of these celestial invaders; while a soft crooning sound, indicative of utter contentment, or as Professor Nestlé of the Milky Ray has more prosaically explained it, due to expiration of air preparatory to the suctional operation involved in the use of the Red Weed, added an indescribable glamour to the enchantment of the scene.

Humiliating as it may seem to the scientific reader, I found it impossible to maintain a Platonic attitude any longer; and applying my mouth to the embouchure of the pipette, warbled faintly in an exquisite falsetto :

" Ulat tanalareezul Savourneen

Dheelish tradioun marexil Vi-Koko for the hair. I want yer, ma honey."

The effect was nothing short of magical. The rhythmic exhalations ceased instanteously, and the tallest and most fluorescent of the Wenuses, laying aside her Red Weed, replied in a low voice thrilling with kinetic emotion:

"Phreata mou sas agapo!"

The sentiment of these remarks was unmistakable, though to my shame I confess I was unable to fathom their meaning, and I was on the point of opening the scullery door and rushing out to declare myself, when I heard a loud banging from the front of the house.

I stumbled up the kitchen stairs, hampered considerably by my wife's skirt; and, by the time I had reached the hall, recognised the raucous accents of Professor Tibbles, the Classical Examiner, shouting in excited tones:

"Let me in, let me in!"

I opened the door as far as it would go without unfastening the chain, and the Professor at once thrust in his head, remaining jammed in the aperture.

"Let me in!" he shouted. "I'm the only man in London besides yourself that hasn't been pulped by the Mash-Glance."

He then began to jabber lines from the classics, and examples from the Latin grammar.

A sudden thought occurred to me. Perhaps he might translate the observation of the Wenus. Should I use him as an interpreter? But a moment's reflection served to convince me of the danger of such a plan. The Professor, already exacerbated by the study of the humanities, was in a state of acute erethism. I thought of the curate, and, maddened by the recollection of all I had suffered, drew the bread-knife from my waist-belt, and shouting, "Go to join your dead languages!" stabbed him up to the maker's name in the semilunar ganglion. His head drooped, and he expired.

I stood petrified, staring at his glazing eyes; then, turning to make for the scullery, was confronted by the catastrophic apparition of the tallest Wenus gazing at me with reproachful eyes and extended tentacles. Disgust at my cruel act and horror at my extraordinary habiliments were written all too plainly in her seraphic lineaments. At least, so I thought. But it turned out to be otherwise; for the

The Death of the Examiner.

Wenus produced from behind her superlatively radiant form a lump of slate which she had extracted from the coal-box.

"Decepti estis, O Puteoli!" she said.

"I beg your pardon," I replied; "but I fail to grasp your meaning."

"She means," said the Examiner, raising himself for another last effort, "that it is time you changed your coal merchant," and so saying he died again.

I was thunderstruck: the Wenuses understood coals!

And then I ran; I could stand it no

longer. The game was up, the cosmic game for which I had laboured so long and strenuously, and with one despairing yell of "Ulla! Ulla!" I unfastened the chain, and, leaping over the limp and prostrate form of the unhappy Tibbles, fled darkling down the deserted street.

II.

THE MAN AT UXBRIDGE ROAD.

AT the corner a happy thought struck me: the landlord of the "Dog and Measles" kept a motor car. I found him in his bar and killed him. Then I broke open the stable and let loose the motor car. It was very restive, and I had to pat it. "Goo' Tea Rose," I said soothingly, "goo' Rockefeller, then." It became quiet, and I struck a match and started the paraffinalia, and in a moment we were under weigh.

I am not an expert motist, although at school I was a fairly good hoop-driver, and the pedestrians I met and overtook had a bad time. One man said, as he bound up a punctured thigh, that the Heat Ray of the Martians was nothing compared with me. I was moting towards Leatherhead, where my cousin lived, when the streak of light caused by the Third Crinoline curdled the paraffin tank. Vain was it to throw water on the troubled oil; the mischief was done. Meanwhile a storm broke. The lightning flashed, the rain beat against my face, the night was exceptionally dark, and to add to my difficulties the motor took the wick between its teeth and fairly bolted.

No one who has never seen an automobile during a spasm of motor ataxy can have any idea of what I suffered. I held the middle of the way for a few yards, but just opposite Uxbridge Road Station I turned the wheel hard a-port, and the motor car overturned. Two men sprang from nowhere, as men will, and sat on its occiput, while I crawled into Uxbridge Road Station and painfully descended the stairs.

I found the platform empty save for a colony of sturdy little newsboys, whose stalwart determination to live filled me with admiration, which I was enjoying until a curious sibillation beneath the bookstall stirred me with panic.

Suddenly, from under a bundle of *British Weeklies*, there emerged a head, and gradually a man crawled out. It was the Artilleryman.

"I'm burning hot," he said; "it's a touch of—what is it?—erethism."

His voice was hoarse, and his Remarks, like the Man of Kent's, were Rambling.

"Where do you come from?" he said.

"I come from Woking," I replied,

"and my nature is Wobbly. I love my love with a W because she is Woluptuous. I took her to the sign of the Wombat and read her *The War of the Worlds*, and treated her to Winkles, Winolia and Wimbos. Her name is Wenus, and she comes from the Milky Way."

He looked at me doubtfully, then shot out a pointed tongue.

"It is you," he said, "the man from Woking. The Johnny what writes for *Nature*. By the way," he interjected, "don't you think some of your stuff is too—what is it?—esoteric? The man," he continued, "as killed the curate in the last book. By the way, it *was* you as killed the curate?"

"Artilleryman," I replied, "I cannot tell a lie. I did it with my little meat-chopper. And you, I presume, are the Artilleryman who attended my lectures on the Eroticism of the Elasmobranch?"

"That's me," he said; "but Lord, how you've changed. Only a fortnight ago, and now you're stone-bald!"

I stared, marvelling at his gift of perception.

"What have you been living on?" I asked.

"Oh," he said, "immature potatoes and Burgundy" (I give the catalogue so precisely because it has nothing to do with the story), "uncooked steak and limp lettuces, precocious carrots and Bartlett pears, and thirteen varieties of fluid beef, which I cannot name except at the usual advertisement rates."

"But can you sleep after it?" said I.

"Blimy! yes," he replied; "I'm fairly —what is it?—eupeptic."

"It's all over with mankind," I muttered.

"It *is* all over," he replied. "The Wenuses 'ave only lost one Crinoline, just one, and they keep on coming; they're falling somewhere every night. Nothing's to be done. We're beat!"

I made no answer. I sat staring, pulverised by the colossal intellectuality of this untutored private. He had attended only three of my lectures, and had never taken any notes.

"This isn't a war," he resumed; "it never was a war. These 'ere Wenuses they wants to be Mas, that's the long and the short of it. Only——"

"Yes?" I said, more than ever impressed by the man's pyramidal intuition.

"They can't stand the climate. They're too—what is it?—exotic."

We sat staring at each other.

"And what will they do?" I humbly

asked, grovelling unscientifically at his feet.

"That's what I've been thinking," said the gunner. "I ain't an ornamental soldier, but I've a good deal of cosmic kinetic optimism, and it's the cosmic kinetic optimist what comes through. Now these Wenuses don't want to wipe *us* all out. It's the women they want to exterminate. They want to collar the men, and you'll see that after a bit they'll begin catching us, picking the best, and feeding us up in cages and men-coops."

"Good heavens!" I exclaimed; "but you *are* a man of genius indeed," and I flung my arms around his neck.

"Steady on!" he said; "don't be so—what is it?—ebullient."

"And what then?" I asked, when my emotion had somewhat subsided.

"Then," said he, "the others must be wary. You and I are mean little cusses: we shall get off. They won't want *us*. And what do we do? Take to the drains!" He looked at me triumphantly.

Quailing before his glory of intellect, I fainted.

"Are you sure?" I managed to gasp, on recovering consciousness.

The Man at Uxbridge Road.

"Yes," he said, "sewer. The drains are the places for you and me. Then we shall play cricket—a narrow drain makes a wonderful pitch—and read the good books—not poetry swipes, and stuff like that, but good books. That's where men like you come in. Your books are the sort: *The Time Machine*, and *Round the World in Eighty Days*, *The Wonderful Wisit*, and *From the Earth to the Moon*, and——"

"Stop!" I cried, nettled at his stupidity. "You are confusing another author and myself."

"Was I?" he said, "that's rum, but I always mix you up with the man you admire so much—Jools Werne. And," he added with a sly look, "you *do* admire him, don't you?"

In a flash I saw the man plain. He was a critic. I knew my duty at once: I must kill him. I did not want to kill him, because I had already killed enough—the curate in the last book, and the Examiner and the landlord of the "Dog and Measles" in this,—but an author alone with a critic in deserted London! What else could I do?

He seemed to divine my thought.

"There's some immature champagne in the cellar," he said.

"No," I replied, thinking aloud; "too slow, too slow."

He endeavoured to pacify me.

"Let me teach you a game," he said.

He taught me one—he taught me several. We began with "Spadille," we ended with "Halma" and "Snap," for parliament points. That is to say, instead of counters we used M.Ps. Grotesque and foolish as this will seem to the sober reader, it is absolutely true. Strange mind of man! that, with our species being mashed all around, we could sit following the chance of this painted pasteboard.

Afterwards we tried "Tiddleywinks"

and "Squails," and I beat him so persistently that both sides of the House were mine and my geniality entirely returned. He might have been living to this hour had he not mentioned something about the brutality of *The Island of Dr. Moreau.* That settled it. I had heard that absurd charge once too often, and raising my Blaisdell binaural stethoscope I leaped upon him. With one last touch of humanity, I turned the orbicular ivory plate towards him and struck him to the earth.

At that moment fell the Fourth Crinoline.

III.

THE TEA-TRAY IN WESTBOURNE GROVE.

MY wife's plan of campaign was simple but masterly. She would enlist an army of enormous bulk, march on the Wenuses in Westbourne Grove, and wipe them from the face of the earth.

Such was my wife's project. My wife's first step was to obtain, as the nucleus of attack, those women to whom the total loss of men would be most disastrous. They flocked to my wife's banner, which was raised in Regent's Park, in front of the pavilion where tea is provided by a maternal County Council.

My mother, who joined the forces and therefore witnessed the muster, tells me it was a most impressive sight. My wife, in a nickel-plated Russian blouse, trimmed with celluloid pompons, aluminium pantaloons, and a pair of Norwegian *Skis*, looked magnificent.

An old Guard, primed with recent articles from the *Queen* by Mrs. Lynn Linton, marched in a place of honour;

The Tea-Tray in Westbourne Grove.

and a small squadron of confirmed misogynists, recruited from the Athenæum, the Travellers' and the Senior United Service Clubs, who professed themselves to be completely Mash-proof, were in charge of the ambulance. The members of the Ladies' Kennel Club, attended by a choice selection of carefully-trained Chows, Schipperkes, Whippets and Griffons, garrisoned various outposts.

The Pioneers joined my wife's ranks with some hesitation. The prospects of a world depleted of men did not seem (says my mother) to fill them with that consternation which was evident in my wife and her more zealous lieutenants. But after a heated discussion at the Club-house, which was marked by several resignations, it was decided to join in the attack. A regiment of Pioneers therefore, marching to the battle-chant of Walt Whitman's "Pioneers, O Pioneers!" brought up (says my mother) the rear.

The march of my wife's troops was a most impressive sight. Leaving Regent's Park by the Clarence Gate, they passed down Upper Baker Street, along Marylebone Road into Edgware Road. Here the troops divided. One

The Tea-Tray in Westbourne Grove.

detachment hastened to Queen's Road, by way of Praed Street, Craven Road, Craven Hill, Leinster Terrace and the Bayswater Road, with the purpose of approaching Whiteley's from the South; the other half marched direct to Westbourne Grove, along Paddington Green Road to Bishop's Road.

Thus, according to my wife's plan, the Wenuses would be between the two wings of the army and escape would be impossible.

Everything was done as my wife had planned. The two detachments reached their destination almost simultaneously. My wife, with the northern wing, was encamped in Bishop's Road, Westbourne Grove and Pickering Place. My mother, with the southern wing (my wife shrewdly kept the command in the family), filled Queen's Road from Whiteley's to Moscow Road. My mother, who has exquisite taste in armour, had donned a superb Cinque-Cento cuirass, a short Zouave jacket embroidered with sequins, accordion-pleated bloomers, luminous leggings, brown Botticelli boots and one tiger-skin spat.

Between the two hosts was the empty road before the Universal Provider's Emporium. The Wenuses were within the building. By the time my wife's warriors were settled and had completed the renovation of their toilets it was high noon.

My wife had never imagined that any delay would occur: she had expected to engage with the enemy at once and have done with it, and consequently brought no provisions and no protection from the sun, which poured down a great bulk of pitiless beams.

The absence of Wenuses and of any sound betokening their activity was disconcerting. However, my wife thought it best to lay siege to

Whiteley's rather than to enter the establishment.

The army therefore waited.

The heat became intense. My wife and her soldiers began to feel the necessity for refreshment. My wife is accustomed to regular meals. The sun grew in strength as the time went on, and my wife gave the order to sit at ease, which was signalled to my mother. My mother tells me that she was never so pleased in her life.

One o'clock struck; two o'clock; three o'clock; and still no Wenuses. Faint sounds were now audible from the crockery department, and then a hissing, which passed by degrees into a humming, a long, loud droning noise. It resembled as nearly as anything the boiling of an urn at a tea-meeting, and awoke in the breasts of my wife and her army an intense and unconquerable longing for tea, which was accentuated as four o'clock was reached. Still no Wenuses. Another hour dragged wearily on, and the craving for tea had become positively excruciating when five o'clock rang out.

At that moment, the glass doors of the crockery department were flung open, and out poured a procession of

Wenuses smiling, said my mother, with the utmost friendliness, dressed as A.B.C. girls, and bearing trays studded with cups and saucers.

With the most seductive and ingratiating charm, a cup was handed to my wife. What to do she did not for the moment know. " Could such a gift be guileless?" she asked herself. "No." And yet the Wenuses looked friendly. Finally her martial spirit prevailed and my wife repulsed the cup, adjuring the rank and file to do the same. But in vain. Every member of my wife's wing of that fainting army greedily grasped a cup. Alas! what could they know of the deadly Tea-Tray of the Wenuses? Nothing, absolutely nothing, such is the disgraceful neglect of science in our schools and colleges. And so they drank and were consumed.

Meanwhile my mother, at the head of the south wing of the army, which had been entirely overlooked by the Wenuses, stood watching the destruction of my wife's host — a figure petrified with alarm and astonishment. One by one she watched her sisters in arms succumb to the awful Tea-Tray.

Then it was that this intrepid woman rose to her greatest height.

"Come!" she cried to her Amazons. "Come! They have no more tea left. Now is the moment ripe."

With these spirited words, my mother and her troops proceeded to charge down Queen's Road upon the unsuspecting Wenuses.

But they had reckoned without the enemy.

The tumult of the advancing host caught the ear of the Wonderful Wisitors, and in an instant they had extracted glittering cases of their crimson cigarettes from their pockets, and lighting them in the strange fashion I have described elsewhere, they proceeded to puff the smoke luxuriously into the faces of my mother and her comrades.

Alas! little did these gallant females know of the horrible properties of the Red Weed. How could they, with our science-teaching in such a wretched state?

The smoke grew in volume and density, spread and spread, and in a few minutes the south wing of my wife's army was as supine as the north.

How my wife and mother escaped I shall not say. I make a point of never explaining the escape of my wife, whether from Martians or Wenuses;

but that night, as Commander-in-Chief, she issued this cataleptic despatch:

> "The Wenuses are able to paralyse all but strong-minded women with their deadly Tea-Tray. Also they burn a Red Weed, the smoke of which has smothered our troops in Westbourne Grove. No sooner have they despoiled Whiteley's than they will advance upon Jay's and Marshall and Snelgrove's. It is impossible to stop them. There is no safety from the Tea-Tray and the Red Weed but in instant flight."

That night the world was again lit by a pale pink flash of light. It was the Fifth Crinoline.

IV.

WRECKAGE.

THE general stampede that ensued on the publication of my wife's despatch is no fit subject for the pen of a coherent scientific writer. Suffice it to say, that in the space of twenty-four hours London was practically empty, with the exception of the freaks at Barnum's, the staff of *The Undertakers' Gazette*, and Mrs. Elphinstone (for that, *pace* Wilkie Collins, was the name of the Woman in White), who would listen to no reasoning, but kept calling upon "George," for that was the name o my cousin's man, who had been in the service of Lord Garrick, the Chief Justice, who had succumbed to dipsomania in the previous invasion.

Meantime the Wenuses, flushed with their success in Westbourne Grove, had carried their devastating course in a south-easterly direction, looting Marshall and Snelgrove's, bearing away the entire stock of driving-gloves from Sleep's and subjecting Redfern's to the asphyxiating fumes of the Red Weed.

It is calculated that they spent nearly two days in Jay's, trying on all the costumes in that establishment, and a week in Peter Robinson's. During these days I never quitted Uxbridge Road Station, for just as I was preparing to leave, my eye caught the title on the bookstall of Grant Allen's work, *The Idea of Evolution!* and I could not stir from the platform until I had skimmed it from cover to cover.

Wearily mounting the stairs, I then turned my face westward. At the corner of Royal Crescent, just by the cabstand, I found a man lying in the roadway. His face was stained with the Red Weed, and his language was quite unfit for the columns of *Nature*.

I applied a limp lettuce to his fevered brow, took his temperature with my theodolite, and pressing a copy of *Home Chat* into his unresisting hand, passed on with a sigh. I think I should have stayed with him but for the abnormal obtusity of his facial angle.

Turning up Clarendon Road, I heard the faint words of the Wenusberg music by Wagner from a pianoforte in the second story of No. 34. I stepped quickly into a jeweller's shop across the road, carried off eighteen immature carats from a tray on the counter, and pitched them through the open window at the invisible pianist. The music ceased suddenly.

It was when I began to ascend Notting Hill that I first heard the hooting. It reminded me at first of a Siren, and then of the top note of my maiden aunt, in her day a notorious soprano vocalist. She subsequently emigrated to France, and entered a nunnery under the religious name of Sœur Marie Jeanne. "Tul-ulla-lulla-liety," wailed the Voice in a sort of superhuman jodel, coming, as it seemed to me, from the region of Westminster Bridge.

The persistent ululation began to get

upon my nerves. I found, moreover, that I was again extremely hungry and thirsty. It was already noon. Why was I wandering alone in this derelict city, clad in my wife's skirt and my cook's Sunday bonnet?

Grotesque and foolish as it may seem to the scientific reader, I was entirely unable to answer this simple conundrum. My mind reverted to my school days. I found myself declining *musa*. Curious to relate, I had entirely forgotten the genitive of *ego*. . . . With infinite trouble I managed to break into a vegetarian restaurant, and made a meal off some precocious haricot beans, a brace of Welsh rabbits, and ten bottles of botanic beer.

Working back into Holland Park Avenue and thence keeping steadily along High Street, Notting Hill Gate, I determined to make my way to the Marble Arch, in the hopes of finding some fresh materials for my studies in the Stone Age.

In Bark Place, where the Ladies' Kennel Club had made their vast grand-stand, were a number of pitiful vestiges of the Waterloo of womenkind. There was a shattered Elswick bicycle, about sixteen yards and a half of nun's veiling, and fifty-three tortoiseshell side-combs. I gazed on the *débris* with apathy mingled with contempt. My movements were languid, my plans of the vaguest. I knew that I wished to avoid my wife, but had no clear idea how the avoiding was to be done.

V.

BUBBLES.

FROM Orme Square, a lean-faced, unkempt and haggard waif, I drifted to Great Orme's Head and back again. Senile dementia had already laid its spectral clutch upon my wizened cerebellum when I was rescued by some kindly people, who tell me that they found me scorching down Hays Hill on a cushion-tired ordinary. They have since told me that I was singing " My name is John Wellington Wells, Hurrah!" and other snatches from a pre-Wenusian opera.

These generous folk, though severely harassed by their own anxieties, took me in and cared for me. I was a lonely man and a sad one, and they bored me. In spite of my desire to give public expression to my gratitude, they have refused to allow their names to appear in these pages, and they consequently enjoy the proud prerogative of being the only anonymous persons in this book. I stayed with them at the Bath Club for four days, and with tears parted from them on the spring-board. They would have kept me for ever, but that would have interfered with my literary plans. Besides, I had a morbid desire to gaze on the Wenuses once more.

And so I went out into the streets again, guided by the weird Voice, and *viâ* Grafton Street, Albemarle Street, the Royal Arcade, Bond Street, Burlington Gardens, Vigo Street and Sackville Street, Piccadilly, Regent Street, Pall Mall East, Cockspur Street and Whitehall, steadily wheeled my way across Westminster Bridge.

There were few people about and their skins were all yellow. Lessing, presumably in his *Laocoon*, has attributed this to the effects of sheer panic; but

Carver's explanation, which attributes the ochre-like tint to the hypodermic operation of the Mash - Glance, seems far more plausible. For myself I abstain from casting the weight of my support in either scale, because my particular province is speculative philosophy and not comparative dermatology.

As I passed St. Thomas's Hospital, the tullululation grew ever louder and louder. At last the source of the sound could no longer be disguised. It proceeded without doubt from the interior of some soap works just opposite Doulton's. The gate was open and a faint saponaceous exhalation struck upon my dilated nostrils. I have always been peculiarly susceptible to odours, though my particular province is not Osmetics but speculative philosophy, and I at once resolved to enter. Leaning my bicycle against the wall of the archway, I walked in, and was immediately confronted by the object of my long search. There, grouped picturesquely round a quantity of large tanks, stood the Wenuses, blowing assiduously through pellucid pipettes and simultaneously chanting in tones of unearthly gravity a strain poignantly suggestive of baffled hopes, thwarted aspirations and impending departure. So absorbed were they in their strange preparations, that they were entirely unconscious of my presence. Grotesque and foolish as this may seem to the infatuated reader, it is absolutely true.

Gradually from out the troubled surface of the tanks there rose a succession of transparent iridescent globules, steadily waxing in bulk until they had attained a diameter of about sixteen feet. The Wenuses then desisted from their labours of inflation, and suddenly plunging into the tanks, reappeared *inside* these opalescent globules. I can only repeat that speculative philosophy, and not sapoleaginous hydrodynamics, is my particular forte, and would refer doubtful readers, in search of further information, to the luminous hypothesis advanced by Professor Cleaver of Washington to account for the imbullification of the Wenuses.[1]

Never shall I forget the touching scene that now unfolded itself before my

[1] Cleaver in a subsequent Memoir [Sonnenschein, London, pp. xiv., 954, 20 in. × 8½, price £2 2s. net] has made out, reluctantly and against the judgment of his firm, that the basic material of the globules, the peculiar tenacity of which was due to some toughening ingredient imported by the Wisitors from their planet, was undoubtedly that indispensable domestic article which is alleged to "save rubbing."

bewildered eyes. Against a back ground of lemon-coloured sky, with the stars shedding their spiritual lustre through the purple twilight, these gorgeous creatures, each ensphered in her beatific bubble, floated tremulously upward on the balmy breeze. In a moment it all flashed upon me. They were passing away from the scene of their brief triumph, and I, a lonely and dejected scientist, saw myself doomed to expiate a moment's madness in long years of ineffectual speculation on the probable development of Moral Ideas.

My mind reverted to my abandoned arguments, embodied in the article which lay beneath the selenite paperweight in my study in Campden Hill Gardens. Frenzied with despair, I shot out an arm to arrest the upward transit of the nearest Wenus, when a strange thing occurred.

"At last!" said a voice.

I was startled. It was my wife, accompanied by Mrs. Elphinstone, my cousin's man, my mother, the widow of the landlord of the "Dog and Measles," Master Herodotus Tibbles in deep mourning, and the Artilleryman's brother from Beauchamp's little livery stables.

I shot an appealing glance to the

disappearing Wenus. She threw me a kiss. I threw her another.

My wife took a step forward, and put her hand to my ear. I fell.

APPENDIX A.

APPENDIX A.

MY mother, whose vigilance during the Wenuses' invasion has been throughout of the greatest assistance to me, kept copies of the various papers of importance which commented upon that event. From them I am enabled, with my mother's consent, to supplement the allusions to contemporary journalism in the body of my history with the following extracts:—

The *Times*, or, as it is better known,

the Thunder Child of Printing House Square, said:

"The Duke of Curzon's statesmanlike reply in the House of Lords last night to the inflammatory question or string of questions put by Lord Ashmead with reference to our planetary visitors will go far to mitigate the unreasoning panic which has laid hold of a certain section of the community. As to the methods by which it has been proposed to confront and repel the invaders, the Duke's remark, 'that the use of dynamite violated the chivalrous instincts which were at the root of the British Nature,' called forth loud applause. The Foreign

Secretary, however, showed that, while deprecating senseless panic, he was ready to take any reasonable steps to allay the natural anxiety of the public, and rising later on in the evening, he announced that a Royal Commission had been appointed, on which Lord Ashmead, Dr. Joseph Parker (of the City Temple), and Mr. Hall Caine, representing the Isle of Man, had consented to serve, and would be dispatched without delay to Kensington Gardens to inquire into the cause of the visit, and, if possible, to induce the new comers to accept an invitation to tea on the Terrace. By way of supplementing these tranquillizing assurances, we may add that we have the authority of the best scientific experts, including Dr. Moreau, Professor Sprudelkopf of Carlsbad, and Dr. Fountain Penn of Philadelphia, for asserting that no animate beings could survive their transference from the atmosphere of Venus to that of our planet for more than fourteen days. It is to be hoped, therefore, that the members of the Royal Commission may be successful in impressing upon our aërial visitors the imperative necessity of a speedy return. In these negotiations it is anticipated that the expressive pantomime of Dr.

Parker, and Mr. Hall Caine's mastery of the Manx dialect, will be of the greatest possible assistance."

To the *Daily Telegraph* Sir Edwin Arnold contributed a poem entitled "Aphrodite Anadyomené; or, Venus at the Round Pond." My mother can remember only the last stanza, which ran as follows:

> "Though I fly to *Fushiyama*,
> Steeped in opalescent *Karma*,
> I shall ne'er forget my charmer,
> My adorable *Khansamah*.
> Though I fly to Tokio,
> Where the sweet *chupatties* blow,
> I shall ne'er forget thee, no!
> *Yamagata, daimio*."

A shilling testimonial to the Wenuses was also started by the same journal, in accordance with the precedent furnished by the similar treatment of the Graces, and an animated controversy raged in its correspondence columns with reference to mixed bathing at Margate, and its effect on the morality of the Wenuses.

A somewhat painful impression was created by the publication of an interview with a well-known dramatic critic in the periodical known as *Great Scott's Thoughts*. This eminent authority gave it as his unhesitating opinion that the Wenuses were not fit persons to associ-

Appendix A.

ate with actors, actresses, or dramatic critics, and that if, as was announced, they had been engaged at Covent Garden to lend realistic verisimilitude to the Venusberg scene in *Tannhäuser*, it was his firm resolve to give up his long crusade against Ibsen, emigrate to Norway, and change his name to that of John Gabriel Borkman. A prolonged sojourn in Poppyland, however, resulted in the withdrawal of this dreadful threat, and, some few weeks after the extinction of the Wenuses, his reconciliation with the dramatic profession was celebrated at a public meeting, where, after embracing all the actor-managers in turn, he was presented by them with a magnificent silver butter-boat, filled to the brim with melted butter ready for immediate use.

APPENDIX B.

APPENDIX B.

MY mother has obtained permission from the Laureate's publishers to reprint the following stanzas from "The Pale Pink Raid":—

"Wrong? O of course it's heinous,
　But we're going, girls, you just bet!
Do they think that the Wars of Wenus
　Can be stopped by an epithet?
When the henpecked Earth-men pray us
　To join them at afternoon tea,
Not rhyme nor reason can stay us
　From flying to set them free.

　　　*　　*　　*

When the men on that hapless planet,
　　Handsome and kind and true,
Cry out, "Hurry up!" O hang it!
　　What else can a Wenus do?
I suppose it was rather bad form, girls,
　　But really we didn't care,
For our planet was growing too warm, girls,
　　And we wanted a change of air.

*　　　*　　　*

Mrs. Grundy may go on snarling,
　　But still, at the Judgment Day,
The author of *England's Darling*
　　I think won't give us away.
We failed, but we chose to chance it,
　　And as one of the beaten side,
I'd rather have made that transit
　　Than written *Jameson's Ride!*"

THE END.

Arrowsmith's 3/6 Series.

Crown 8vo, cloth.

Vol.	Title	Author
I.	THREE MEN IN A BOAT (To Say Nothing of the Dog)	Jerome K. Jerome.
II.	THE END OF A LIFE	Eden Phillpotts.
III.	DIARY OF A PILGRIMAGE	Jerome K. Jerome.
IV.	RECALLED TO LIFE	Grant Allen.
V.	A FRENCHMAN IN AMERICA	Max O'Rell.
VI.	THE SUPERNATURAL?	L. A. Weatherly AND J. N. Maskelyne.
VII.	THE WHITE HAT	Finch Mason.
VIII.	FIFTY POUNDS FOR A WIFE	A. L. Glyn.
IX.	A TIGER'S CUB	Eden Phillpotts.
X.	WHEN I LIVED IN BOHEMIA	Fergus Hume.
XI.	THE DIARY OF A NOBODY	George Grossmith AND Weedon Grossmith.
XII.	FLYING VISITS	Harry Furniss.
XIII.	"LIFE IN HIM YET"	Henry St. John Raikes.
XIV.	DR. PAULL'S THEORY	Mrs. A. M. Diehl.
XV.	CLAUD BRENNAN	John Ferrars.
XVI.	THE GREAT SHADOW and BEYOND THE CITY	Conan Doyle.
XVII.	THREE BRACE OF LOVERS	Harold Vallings.
XVIII.	THE PRISONER OF ZENDA	Anthony Hope.
XIX.	NEIGHBOURS OF OURS	Henry W. Nevinson.
XX.	STATION STORIES	Murray Cator.
XXI.	PETER STEELE, THE CRICKETER	Horace G. Hutchinson.
XXII.	DEAD MAN'S COURT	Maurice H. Hervey.
XXIII.	"NOT EXACTLY"	E. M. Stooke.
XXIV.	MINOR DIALOGUES	W. Pett Ridge.
XXV.	GREENROOM RECOLLECTIONS	Arthur Wm. A'Beckett.
XXVI.	DARTMOOR	Maurice H. Hervey.
XXVII.	THE INDISCRETION OF THE DUCHESS	Anthony Hope.
XXVIII.	A BRIDE'S MADNESS	Allen Upward.
XXIX.	THE SACK OF MONTE CARLO	Walter Frith.
XXX.	LORD DULLBOROUGH	Hon. Stuart Erskine.

Bristol: J. W. ARROWSMITH, 11 Quay Street.
London: SIMPKIN, MARSHALL, HAMILTON, KENT & CO., LIMITED.

Arrowsmith's Bristol Library.

Fcap. 8vo, stiff covers, 1/-; cloth, 1/6.

Saturday Review speaks of ARROWSMITH'S BRISTOL LIBRARY "as necessary to the traveller as a rug in winter and a dust-coat in summer."

1.	CALLED BACK	HUGH CONWAY.
2.	BROWN EYES	MAY CROMMELIN.
3.	DARK DAYS	HUGH CONWAY.
4.	FORT MINSTER, M.P.	Sir E. J. REED, K.C.B., M.P.
5.	THE RED CARDINAL	Mrs. FRANCES ELLIOT.
6.	THE TINTED VENUS	F. ANSTEY.
7.	JONATHAN'S HOME	ALAN DALE.
8.	SLINGS AND ARROWS	HUGH CONWAY.
9.	OUT OF THE MISTS	DANIEL DORMER.
10.	KATE PERCIVAL	Mrs. J. COMYNS CARR.
11.	KALEE'S SHRINE	GRANT ALLEN.
12.	CARRISTON'S GIFT	HUGH CONWAY.
13.	THE MARK OF CAIN	ANDREW LANG.
14.	PLUCK	J. STRANGE WINTER.
15.	DEAR LIFE	Mrs. J. E. PANTON.
16.	GLADYS' PERIL	JOHN COLEMAN and JOHN C. CHUTE.
17.	WHOSE HAND? or, The Mystery of No Man's Heath	W. G. WILLS and The Hon. Mrs. GREENE.
18.	THAT WINTER NIGHT	ROBERT BUCHANAN.
19.	THE GUILTY RIVER	WILKIE COLLINS.
20.	FATAL SHADOWS	Mrs. L. L. LEWIS.
21.	THE LOVELY WANG	Hon. L. WINGFIELD.
22.	PATTY'S PARTNER	JEAN MIDDLEMASS.
23.	"V.R." A Comedy of Errors	EDWARD ROSE.
24.	THE PARK LANE MYSTERY	JOSEPH HATTON.
25.	FRIEND MAC DONALD	MAX O'RELL.
26.	KATHARINE REGINA	WALTER BESANT
27.	JAN VERCLOOTZ	MATTHEW STRONG.
28.	THE CLIFF MYSTERY	HAMILTON AÏDÉ.
29.	AS A BIRD TO THE SNARE	GERTRUDE WARDEN.
30.	TRACKED OUT	ARTHUR À BECKETT.
31.	A SOCIETY CLOWN	GEORGE GROSSMITH
32.	CHECK AND COUNTER-CHECK	BRANDER MATTHEWS and GEORGE H. JESSOP.
33.	THE INNER HOUSE	WALTER BESANT.
34.	A VAGABOND WILL	W. G. WATERS.
35.	PHARAOH'S DAUGHTER	EDGAR LEE.
36.	TROLLOPE'S DILEMMA	ST. AUBYN.
37.	JACQUES BONHOMME	MAX O'RELL.
38.	THE DOUBTS OF DIVES	WALTER BESANT.
39.	FAIR PHYLLIS OF LAVENDER WHARF	JAMES GREENWOOD.
40.	HARD LUCK	ARTHUR À BECKETT.
41.	TWO AND TWO. A Tale of Four	ELIZABETH GLAISTER.
42.	THE RAJAH AND THE ROSEBUD	WILLIAM SIME.
43.	BEHIND THE KAFES	MARY ALBERT.

Bristol: J. W. ARROWSMITH, 11 Quay Street.
London: SIMPKIN, MARSHALL, HAMILTON, KENT & CO. Limited.

Arrowsmith's Bristol Library.

Fcap. 8vo, stiff covers, 1/-; cloth, 1/6.

"Mr. Arrowsmith, since the far-off days when he discovered poor Hugh Conway, has made the public his debtors for many a delightful book."—*Liverpool Post.*

44.	THE DEMONIAC	WALTER BESANT.
45.	OUR BOYS & GIRLS AT SCHOOL.	HENRY J. BARKER, B.A.
46.	THE CORONER'S UNDERSTUDY.	CAPTAIN COE.
47.	A ROMANCE OF THE MOORS	MONA CAIRD.
48.	THE SHIELD OF LOVE	B. L. FARJEON.
49.	A SPINSTER'S DIARY	Mrs. A. PHILLIPS.
50.	THE AVENGING OF HIRAM	BENNETT COLL.
51.	TRAVELLERS' TALES	Edited by E. A. MORTON.
52.	THE GREAT SHADOW	A. CONAN DOYLE.
53.	HARRY FORRESTER, late Blankth	ANNIE THOMAS (Mrs. Pender-Cudlip)
54.	{ A GEM OF CREMONA	B. M. VERE and
	{ A CHEF D'ŒUVRE	E. BLAIR-OLIPHANT.
55.	THE SLAPPING SAL and OTHER TALES	{ A. CONAN DOYLE. VARIOUS AUTHORS.
56.	DECEMBER ROSES	Mrs. CAMPBELL PRAED.
57.	THE TRESPASSER	GILBERT PARKER.
58.	THE TELEPORON and OTHER STORIES	W. H. STACPOOLE.
59.	AT THE SIGN OF THE WICKET	E. B. V. CHRISTIAN.
60.	CONSCIENCE MAKES THE MARTYR	S. M. CRAWLEY-BOEVEY.
61.	AN UNFINISHED MARTYRDOM and OTHER STORIES	A. ST. JOHN ADCOCK.
62.	THE INDISCRETION OF THE DUCHESS	ANTHONY HOPE.
63.	AN APOSTLE OF FREEDOM	EDWIN HUGHES, B.A.
64.	ENGLAND v. AUSTRALIA	J. N. PENTELOW.
65.	THE ADVENTURES OF ARTHUR ROBERTS, by Road, Rail, and River	TOLD BY HIMSELF, and chronicled by RICHARD MORTON.
66.	IN THE SMOKE OF WAR	WALTER RAYMOND.
67.	PENLEY ON HIMSELF.	
68.	TOLD IN THE PAVILION	ALFRED COCHRANE.
69.	HOW'S THAT? Including "A Century of Grace." Verses. Cricket Sketches.	HARRY FURNISS. E. J. MILLIKEN. E. B. V. CHRISTIAN.
70.	MY TERRIBLE TWIN	FRED WHISHAW.
71.	THE RECOVERY OF JANE VERCOE and OTHER STORIES	MABEL QUILLER-COUCH.
72.	THE WIZARD	H. RIDER HAGGARD.
73.	THE COUNTY CRICKET CHAMPIONSHIP	REV. R. S. HOLMES.
74.	THE MILLIONAIRE OF PARKERSVILLE	MARSHALL G. WOOD.
75	PEPITA OF THE PAGODA	TIGHE HOPKINS.
76.	JOTS	GEORGE THORNE.
77.	A DAUGHTER OF ASTREA	E. PHILLIPS OPPENHEIM

Bristol: J. W. ARROWSMITH, 11 Quay Street.
London: SIMPKIN, MARSHALL, HAMILTON, KENT & Co., Limited.

www.ingramcontent.com/pod-product-compliance
Lightning Source LLC
LaVergne TN
LVHW092324080426
835508LV00039B/573